My Book of
Words

SOUTHWESTERN
advantage.

© 2014 Southwestern Advantage
Reprinted in 2016
Nashville, Tennessee

Henry Bedford
Chief Executive Officer,
Southwestern/Great American, Inc.

Dan Moore
President, Southwestern Advantage

Curriculum Director
Janet D. Sweet

Art Director
Travis Rader

Production Manager
Powell Ropp

The publisher would also like to thank
the original creators of this book:

Editorial Team
Mary Cummings • Judy Jackson
Barbara J. Reed

Art and Design Team
Steve Newman • Starletta Polster
Matt Carrington

ISBN 978-0-87197-599-7

Printed by RR Donnelley,
Shenzhen, Guangdong, China

Contents

Skwids.com

The Ones That Start Ahead...Stay Ahead!

- Skwids video lessons, games, and quizzes provide the essential skills needed for success in school.

- Skwids tracks progress and tells you what your child knows and what they should focus on next.

- Skwids teaches important life lessons too, for emotionally well-rounded kids.

- Skwids makes learning fun so kids stay engaged in the process at school and at home.

Download the Skwids App! Kids can watch favorite episodes wherever they want, whenever they want!

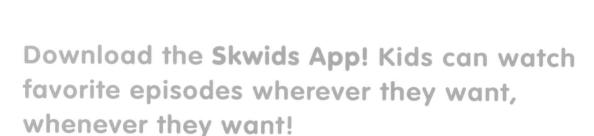

Note to parents

Congratulations on choosing the *My Book* series for nurturing your child's vocabulary development! Learning to read is an exciting time for you and your child, and vocabulary development is an essential first step in early reading success.

Southwestern Advantage understands that young children are naturally drawn to images, words, and ideas that are all about their world. The *My Book of Words* features bright-colored art and vibrant illustrations to encourage your child to explore the familiar, high-interest words and concepts used in everyday life.

Your child will also enjoy the lovable Skwids characters from Southwestern Advantage's early learning website, www.skwids.com, as they introduce each category of vocabulary words. Learn more about Kangaroo, Monkey, Giraffe, and the other Skwids characters as they weave the concepts from the *My Books* series—and other Advantage book series—into fun early-learning videos, games, songs, and more!

We are committed to helping our youngest learners develop early reading success and a zest for learning. So turn the page and enjoy an important step in learning to read!

Janet D. Sweet
Curriculum Director

Wild animals

Wild animals live in nature. What is your favorite wild animal?

elephant

giraffe

bear

snake

frog

kangaroo

giraffe   elephant   bear   snake   frog   kangaroo

lion

monkey

seahorse

gorilla

zebra

alligator

lion monkey gorilla seahorse alligator zebra

Animal homes

Some animals use homes to protect them from danger.

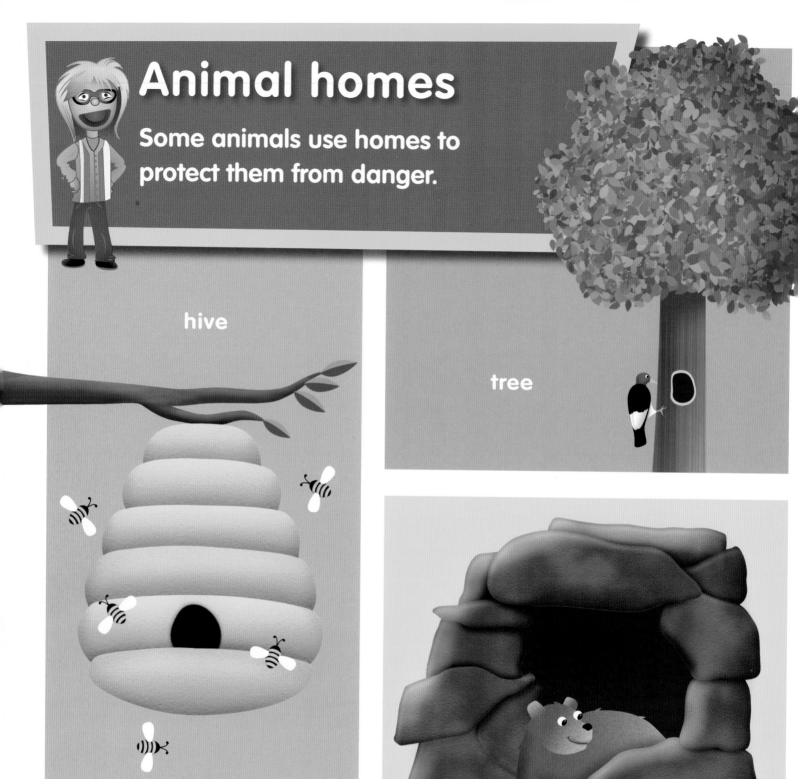

hive

tree

den

8   hive   tree   den

burrow

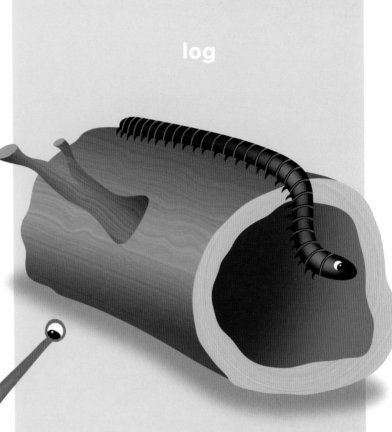

log

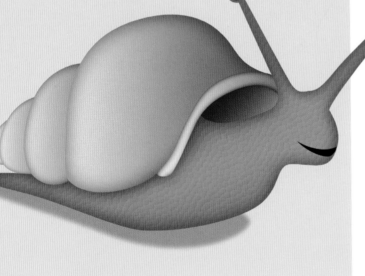

shell

nest

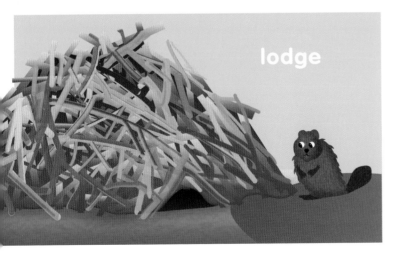

lodge

burrow   shell   log   lodge   nest   **9**

Animal babies

Which animal babies hatch from an egg?

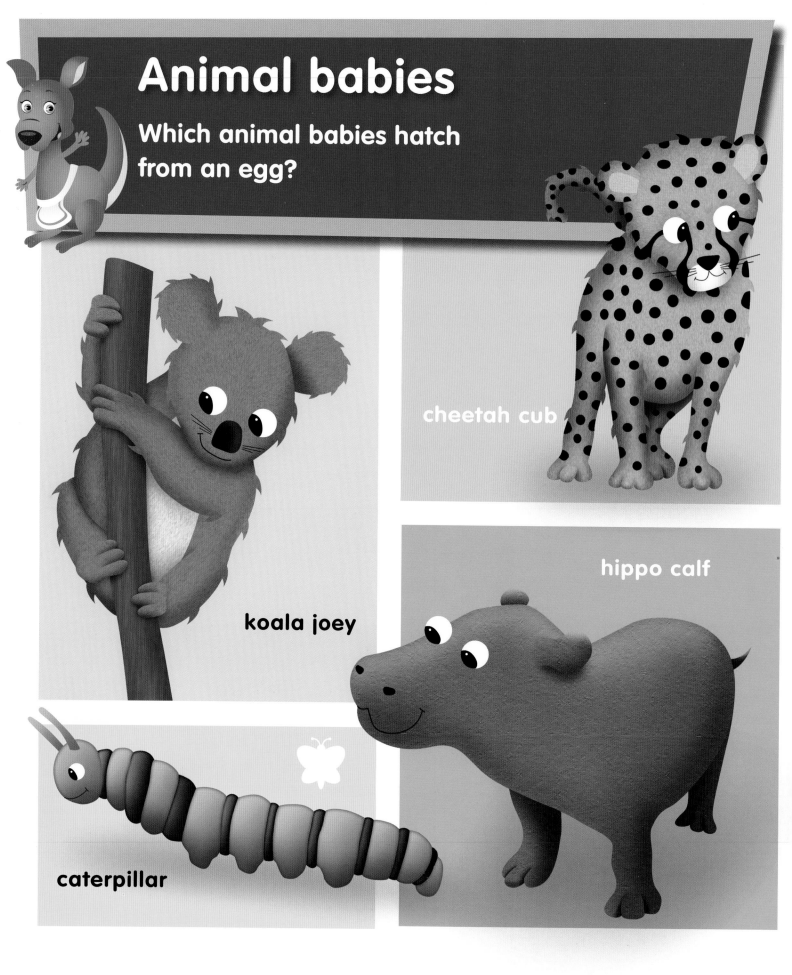

koala joey

cheetah cub

hippo calf

caterpillar

cheetah cub   koala joey   hippo calf   caterpillar

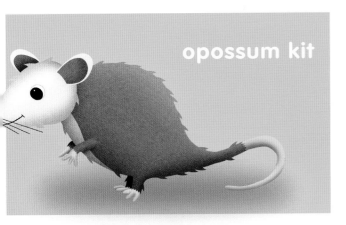

opossum kit

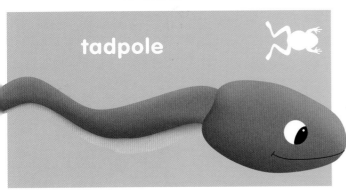

tadpole

panda cub

duckling

bat pup

opossum kit   tadpole   panda cub   bat pup   duckling   **11**

Plants

Plants are living things. Most plants need air, water, sunshine, and soil to grow.

flower

petal

stem

flower   petal   stem

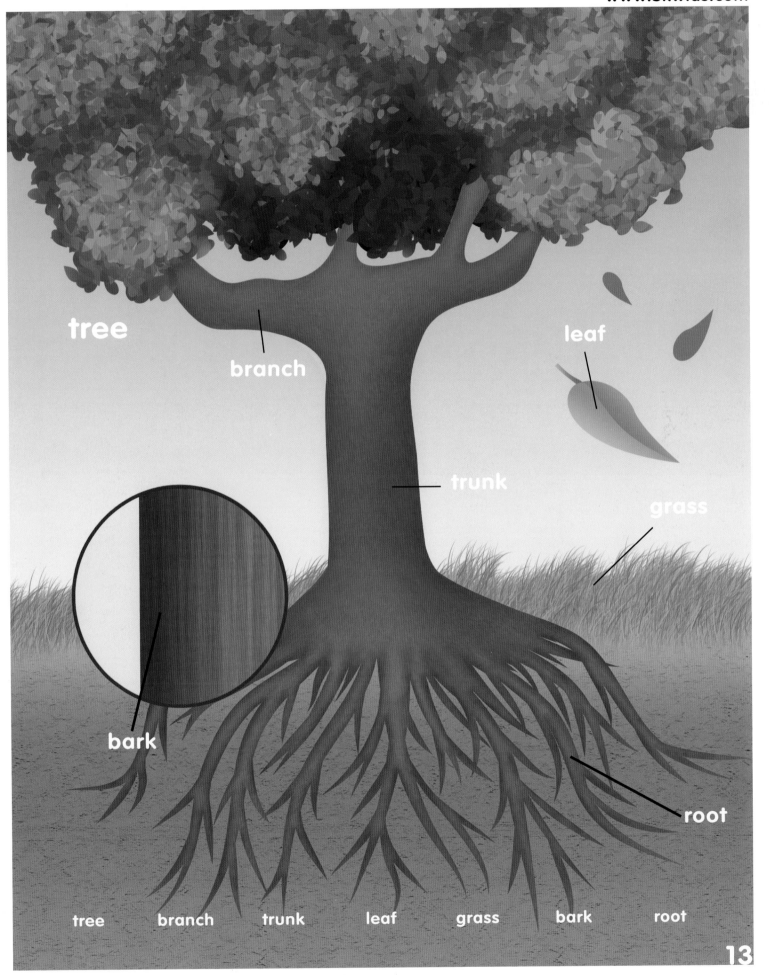

tree

branch

leaf

trunk

grass

bark

root

tree   branch   trunk   leaf   grass   bark   Root

Features of the land

Features of the land come in all shapes and sizes.

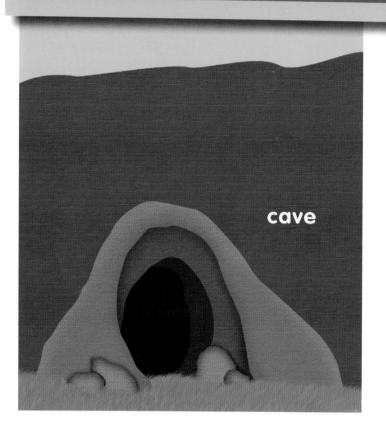

cave

desert

ocean

island

cave   desert   ocean   island

plain

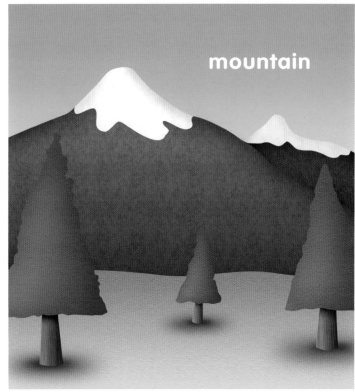

mountain

river

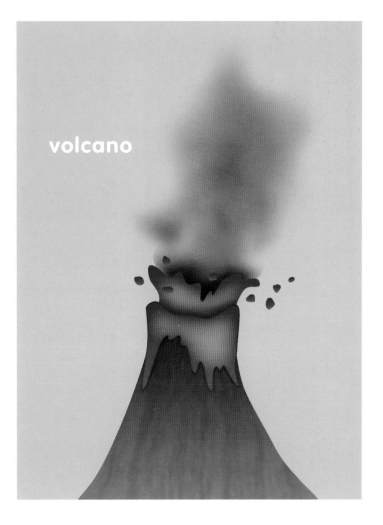

volcano

valley

plain   mountain   river   valley   volcano   **15**

Weather

Weather describes what it is like outside.

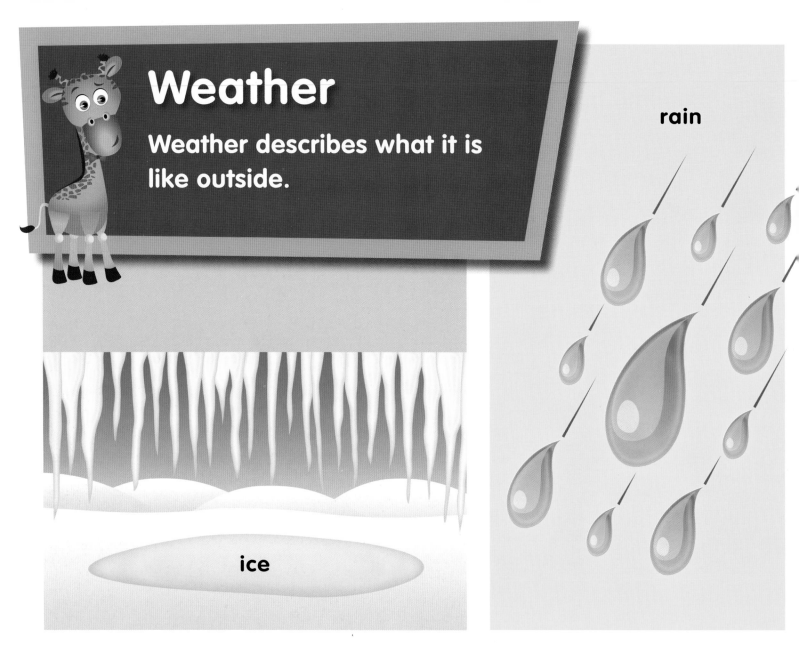

rain

ice

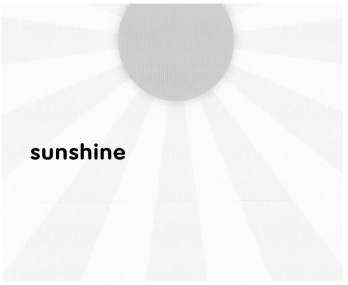

sunshine

fog

rain   ice   sunshine   fog

wind

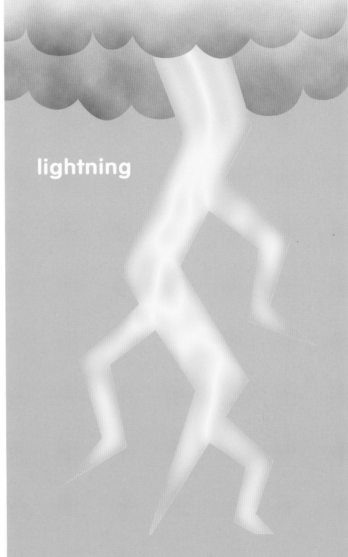

lightning

hail

snow

wind   lightning   hail   snow   **17**

Seasons

Seasons bring changes in weather.

Spring

Summer

Fall

Winter

In a rain forest

Many kinds of plants and animals live in a rain forest.

toucan

jaguar

fern

stream

20

vine

monkey

snake

tree

frog

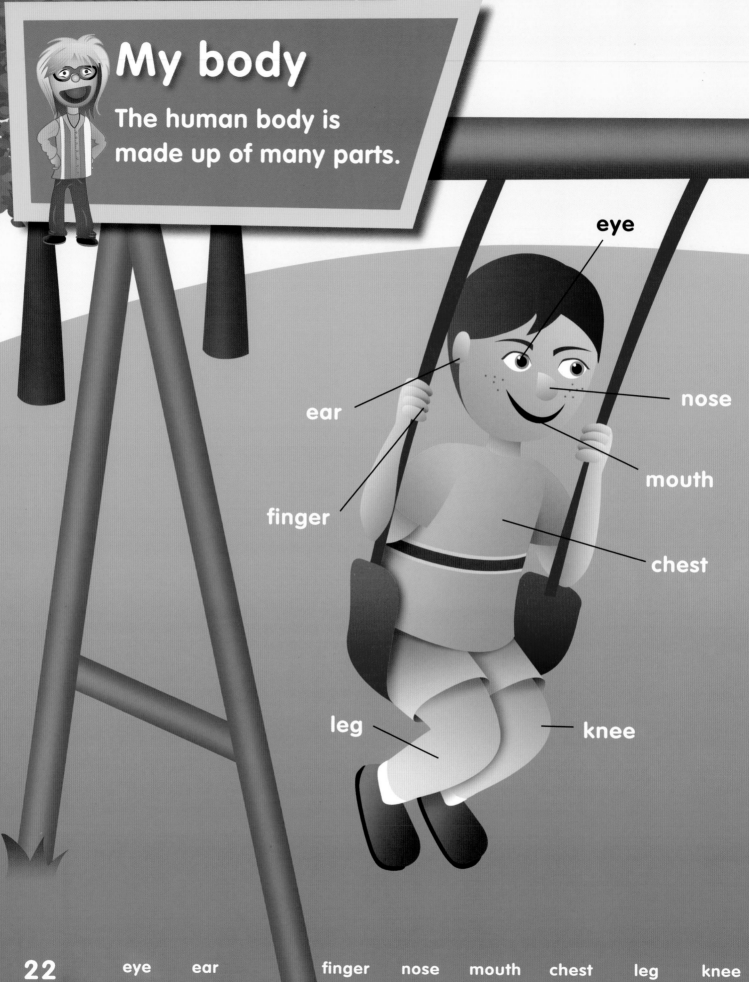

My body

The human body is made up of many parts.

eye

nose

ear

mouth

finger

chest

leg

knee

eye   ear   finger   nose   mouth   chest   leg   knee

hair   head   face   arm   elbow   foot   ankle   toe   **23**

Staying healthy

The pictures on this page show activities that can help you to stay healthy.

drink water

exercise

sleep

24   drink water   exercise   sleep

**Eating from the five food groups
helps the body to stay healthy.**

grains

vegetables

fruit

dairy

protein

Clothing

Clothing helps protect the body. It is also worn for decoration.

mitten

scarf

tie

skirt

hat

shoes

belt

mitten   scarf   tie   skirt   hat   shoes   belt

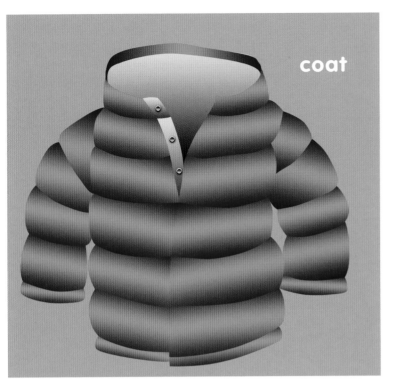

coat

sweater

dress

socks

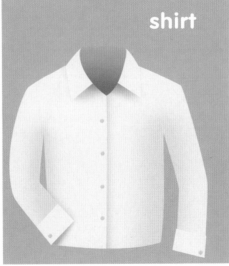

shirt

jeans

coat   sweater   dress   socks   shirt   jeans   **27**

Feelings

Feelings describe how we feel inside.

surprised

happy

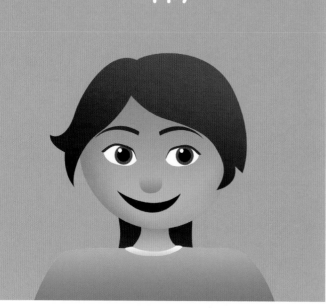

confused

calm

shy

surprised   happy   confused   calm   shy

embarrassed

worried

sad

angry

embarrassed   worried   sad   angry   **29**

Hobbies

Hobbies are things we do for fun.

reading books

playing sports

camping

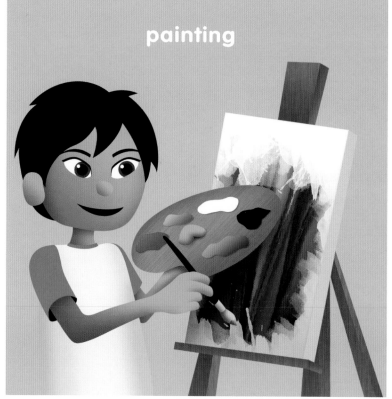

painting

reading books   **playing sports**   **camping**   **painting**

playing games

playing outside

making music

dancing

playing games　　　**playing outside**　　　**making music**　　　**dancing**　　　**31**

Sports

Sports are a great way to have fun and stay healthy.

gymnastics

basketball

swimming

ice hockey

gymnastics   **basketball**   **swimming**   **ice hockey**

skiing

soccer

track

football

ice skating

baseball

skiing soccer track football ice skating baseball **33**

Pets

What is your favorite pet?

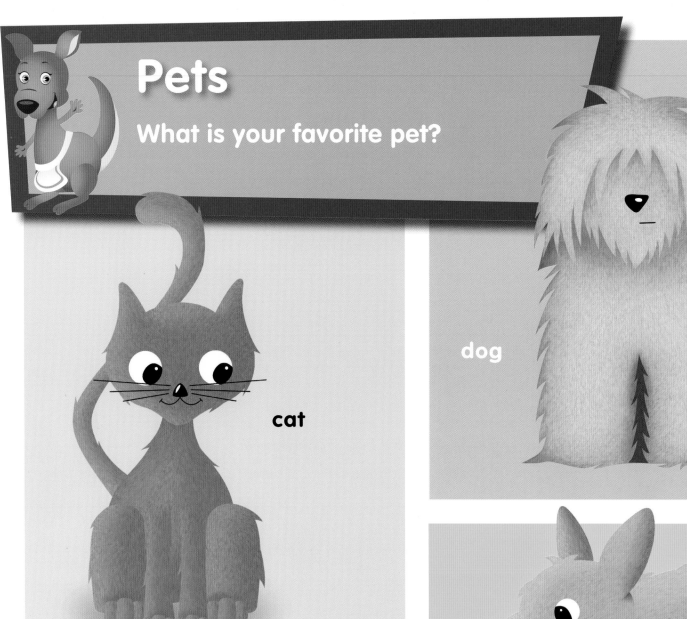

cat

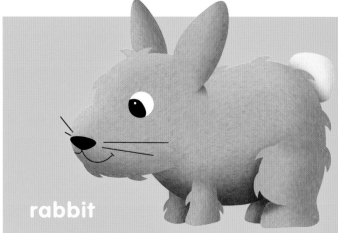

dog

rabbit

gerbil

hamster

cat   dog   gerbil   rabbit   hamster

horse

fish

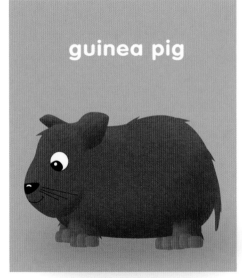

mouse

hermit crab

bird

guinea pig

horse   fish   mouse   hermit crab   bird   guinea pig   **35**

Family members

Families can be large or small.

grandmother

aunt

uncle

nephew

niece

36

father

sister

grandfather

brother

mother

Community helpers

Many people have jobs that help people in the community.

garbage collector

4
+ 2
6

teacher

mail carrier

police officer

nurse

teacher   garbage collector   nurse   mail carrier   police officer

doctor

lawyer

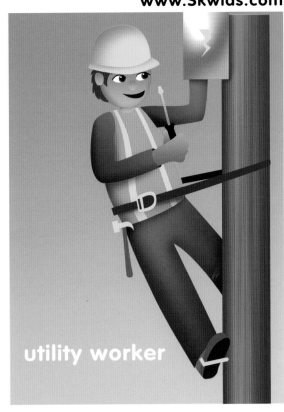

utility worker

firefighter

bus driver

| doctor | lawyer | utility worker | firefighter | bus driver | **39** |

Getting around

People can travel from place to place in many different ways.

bus

motorcycle

rollerblades

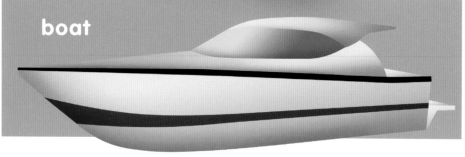

boat

bus   motorcycle   boat   rollerblades

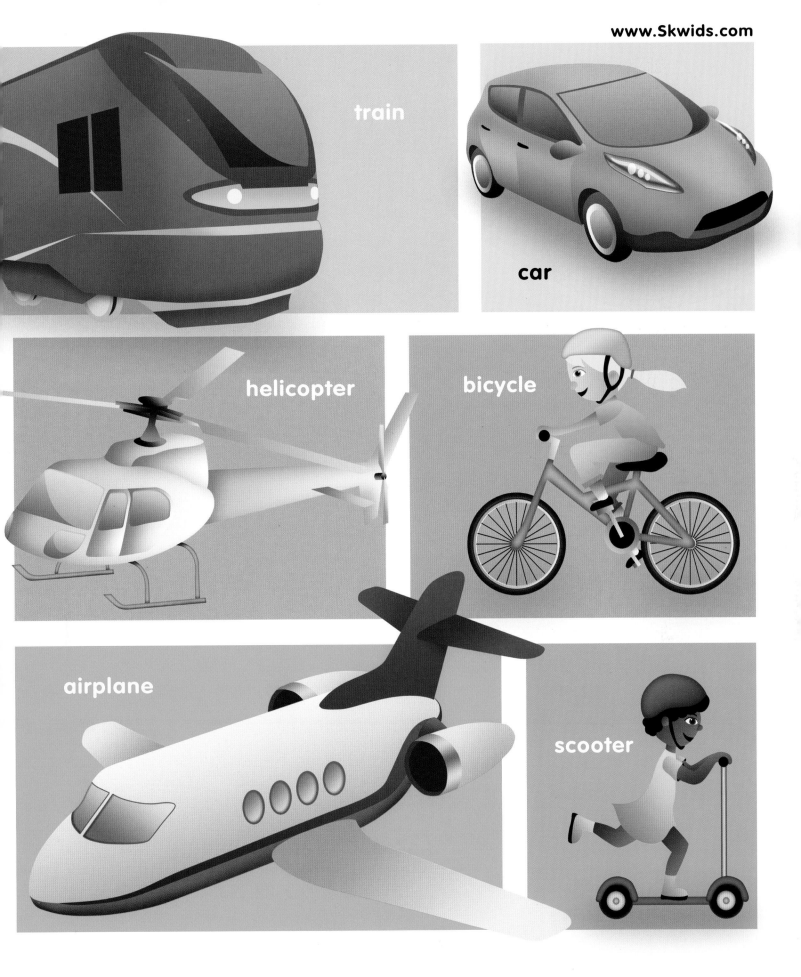

train   car   helicopter   bicycle   airplane   scooter   **41**

Around town

It's a busy day around town! What people and objects do you see?

crossing guard

crosswalk

car

STOP

ladder

firefighters

fire truck

stop sign

vendor

Newspaper Stand

STOP

mother

child

bicycle

Games

The grid on page 45 shows many different shapes and objects. Look carefully at the grid and follow the instructions below.

1. Count the caterpillars.
2. Count the ducklings.
3. Count the cars.
4. Count the skirts.
5. Count the objects that are clothing.
6. Count the baby animals.
7. Count the wild animals.
8. Count the animals that are pets.
9. Count the animals that live in water.
10. Count the things that you find in nature.
11. Count the things that are made by people.
12. Count the things that are orange.
13. Count the things that are yellow.
14. Count the vehicles.
15. Name all of the different objects!

Look again!

These two pictures are not exactly the same. Can you find the eight things that are different in the second picture?

Word-Building activities

As your child's first teacher, you play an important role in nurturing your young learner's vocabulary development, one of the five essential steps that children must master in order to read. Here are some tips for promoting vocabulary development and reading success at home.

- Make reading *My Book of Words* a warm, pleasant experience. Sit close to your child, snuggle, laugh, and have fun as you read aloud. Ask your child what he or she thinks about the pictures, characters, and objects on the pages. Read aloud with expression. Use different voices for the different characters, ask about the details that make the seasons different, and add sound effects for the different vehicles.

- Sing songs, recite rhymes and poems with repeating phrases, tell riddles and knock-knock jokes, and share stories that you enjoyed as a child.

- Make up stories while traveling in the car. Start with a silly beginning sentence, such as "Once upon a time, there was a skunk in our bathtub." Take turns adding new sentences aloud.

- Have your child use as many adjectives as possible to describe a favorite story character, family relative, birthday present, or costume.

- Play a simple rhyming game with your child. Take turns coming up with as many words as possible that rhyme with simple words, such as *school (pool, tool, cool)* or *pin (win, tin, skin)*.

- Notice and talk about road signs, menus, and advertisements with your child when traveling. When at the grocery store, encourage your child to read the letters and words on boxes and cans.

- Choose one of your child's favorite subjects to play a game of "What Am I?" For example, if your child likes animals, you could quack like a duck and ask *What am I?* Or you could say *I am big and gray, and I have a trunk. What am I?* (elephant)

- Talk with your child all the time about subjects that he or she finds interesting. This reinforces his or her understanding of language and helps introduce new vocabulary and concepts.

Activities like these build the necessary groundwork for your child to connect information with printed words. Now your child is ready to take the next step to becoming a reader!